FIRESIDE SERIES

Volume 1, No. 1

Defining
the
Master

DEFINING THE MASTER

JZK Publishing,
A Division of JZK, Inc.

P.O. Box 1210
Yelm, Washington 98597
360.458.5201
800.347.0439
www.ramtha.com
www.jzkpublishing.com

Point Zero

7th level
...consciousness

Infinite Unknown

6th level
...perconsciousness

Gamma Ray

5th level
...rconsciousness

X-Ray

4th level
...dy Consciousness

Ultraviolet Blue

3rd level
...scious Awareness

Visible Light

2nd level
...al Consciousness

Infrared

1st level
...consciousness

Meridian

Sixth Seal
Pineal gland
when energy
penetrates th...
mind (the ...

Fifth Seal
thyroid
living truth ...

Forth Seal
Connected
Gland — ...
of transmutat...
spiritual awa...

Third Seal
Solar ple...
Represents ...

Second Se...
Represents
often affiliat...
procreation ...

First Seal
Represents
and survival...

...ssolve
Seals
...ulate
...aconsciousness

...als
...
...als dissolve
...ality. Seals
...y formulate
...irit body.
...als
...

These series of teachings are designed for all the students of the Great Work who love the teachings of the Ram.

It is suggested that you create an ideal learning environment for study and contemplation.

Light your fireplace and get cozy. Prepare yourself. Open your mind to learn and be genius.

FOREWORD TO THE NEW EDITION

The Fireside Series Collection Library is an ongoing library of the hottest topics of interest taught by Ramtha. These series of teachings are designed for all the students of the Great Work who love the teachings of the Ram. This library collection is also intended as a continuing learning tool for the students of Ramtha's School of Enlightenment and for everyone interested and familiar with Ramtha's teachings. In the last three decades Ramtha has continuously and methodically deepened and expanded his exposition of the nature of reality and its practical application through various disciplines. It is assumed by the publisher that the reader has attended a Beginning Retreat or workshop through Ramtha's School of Enlightenment or is at least familiar with Ramtha's instruction to his beginning class of students. This required information for beginning students is found in *Ramtha: A Beginner's Guide to Creating Reality*, Third Ed. (Yelm: JZK Publishing, a division of JZK, Inc., 2004).

We have included in the Fireside Series a glossary of some of the basic concepts used by Ramtha so the reader can become familiarized with these teachings. We have also included a brief introduction of Ramtha by JZ Knight that describes how all this began. Enjoy your learning and contemplation.

Contents

INTRODUCTION TO RAMTHA
BY JZ KNIGHT

"In other words, his whole point of focus is to come here and to teach you to be extraordinary."

You don't have to stand for me. My name is JZ Knight and I am the rightful owner of this body, and welcome to Ramtha's school, and sit down. Thank you.

So we will start out by saying that Ramtha and I are two different people, beings. We have a common reality point and that is usually my body. I am a lot different than he is. Though we sort of look the same, we really don't look the same.

What do I say? Let's see. All of my life, ever since I was a little person, I have heard voices in my head and I have seen wonderful things that to me in my life were normal. And I was fortunate enough to have a family or a mother who was a very psychic human being, who sort of never condemned what it was that I was seeing. And I had wonderful experiences all my life, but the most important experience was that I had this deep and profound love for God, and there was a part of me that understood what that was. Later in my life I went to church and I tried to understand God from the viewpoint of religious doctrine and had a lot of difficulty with that because it was sort of in conflict with what I felt and what I knew.

Ramtha has been a part of my life ever since I was born, but I didn't know who he was and I didn't know what he was, only that there was a wonderful force that walked with me, and when I was in trouble — and had a lot of pain in my life growing up — that I always had extraordinary experiences with this being who would talk to me. And I could hear him as clearly as I can hear you if we were to have a conversation. And he helped me to understand a lot of things in my life that were sort of beyond the normal scope of what someone would give someone as advice.

It wasn't until 1977 that he appeared to me in my kitchen on a Sunday afternoon as I was making pyramids with my husband at that time, because we were into dehydrating food and we were into hiking and backpacking and all that stuff. And so I put one of these ridiculous things on my head, and at the other end of my kitchen this wonderful apparition appeared that was seven feet tall and glittery and beautiful and stark. You just don't expect at 2:30 in the afternoon that this is going to appear in your kitchen. No one is ever prepared for that. And so Ramtha at that time really made his appearance known to me.

The first thing I said to him — and I don't know where this comes from — was that "You are so beautiful. Who are you?"

And he has a smile like the sun. He is extraordinarily handsome. And he said, "My name is Ramtha the Enlightened One, and I have come to help you over the ditch." Being the simple person that I am, my immediate reaction was to look at the floor because I thought maybe something had happened to the floor, or the bomb was being dropped; I didn't know.

And it was that day forward that he became a constant in my life. And during the year of 1977 a lot of interesting things happened, to say the least. My two younger children at that time got to meet Ramtha and got to experience some incredible phenomena, as well as my husband.

Later that year, after teaching me and having some difficulty telling me what he was and me understanding, one day he said to me, "I am going to send you a runner that will bring you a set of books, and you read them because then you will know what I am." And those books were called the *Life and Teaching of the Masters of the Far East* (DeVorss & Co. Publishers, 1964). And so I read them and I began to understand that Ramtha was one of those beings, in a way. And that sort of took me out of the are-you-the-devil-or-are-you-God sort of category that was plaguing me at the time.

And after I got to understand him, he spent long, long

moments walking into my living room, all seven feet of this beautiful being making himself comfortable on my couch, sitting down and talking to me and teaching me. And what I didn't realize at that particular time was he already knew all the things I was going to ask and he already knew how to answer them. But I didn't know that he knew that.

So he patiently since 1977 has dealt with me in a manner by allowing me to question not his authenticity but things about myself as God, teaching me, catching me when I would get caught up in dogma or get caught up in limitation, catching me just in time and teaching me and walking me through that. And I always said, "You know, you are so patient. You know, I think it is wonderful that you are so patient." And he would just smile and say that he is 35,000 years old, what else can you do in that period of time? So it wasn't really until about ten years ago that I realized that he already knew what I was going to ask and that is why he was so patient. But as the grand teacher that he is, he allowed me the opportunity to address these issues in myself and then gave me the grace to speak to me in a way that was not presumptuous but in a way, as a true teacher would, that would allow me to come to realizations on my own.

Channeling Ramtha since late 1979 has been an experience, because how do you dress your body for — Ram is seven feet tall and he wears two robes that I have always seen him in. Even though they are the same robe, they are really beautiful so you never get tired of seeing them. The inner robe is snow white and goes all the way down to where I presume his feet are, and then he has an overrobe that is beautiful purple. But you should understand that I have really looked at the material on these robes and it is not really material. It is sort of like light. And though the light has a transparency to them, there is an understanding that what he is wearing has a reality to it.

Ramtha's face is cinnamon-colored skin, and that is the best way I can describe it. It is not really brown and it is not really white and it is not really red; it is sort of a blending of that. And he has very deep black eyes that can look into you and you know you are being looked into. He has eyebrows that look like wings of a bird that come high on his brow. He has a very square jaw and a beautiful mouth, and when he smiles you know that you are in heaven. He has long, long hands, long fingers that he uses very eloquently to demonstrate his thought.

Well, imagine then how after he taught me to get out of my body by actually pulling me out and throwing me in the tunnel, and hitting the wall of light, bouncing back, and realizing my kids were home from school and I just got through doing breakfast dishes, that getting used to missing time on this plane was really difficult, and I didn't understand what I was doing and where I was going. So we had a lot of practice sessions.

You can imagine if he walked up to you and yanked you right out of your body and threw you up to the ceiling and said now what does that view look like, and then throwing you in a tunnel — and perhaps the best way to describe it is it is a black hole into the next level — and being flung through this tunnel and hitting this white wall and having amnesia. And you have to understand, I mean, he did this to me at ten o'clock in the morning and when I came back off of the white wall it was 4:30. So I had a real problem in trying to adjust with the time that was missing here. So we had a long time in teaching me how to do that, and it was fun and frolic and absolutely terrifying at moments.

But what he was getting me ready to do was to teach me something that I had already agreed to prior to this incarnation, and that my destiny in this life was not just to marry and to have children and to do well in life but to overcome the adversity to let what was previously planned happen, and that happening including an extraordinary consciousness, which he is.

Trying to dress my body for Ramtha was a joke. I didn't

know what to do. The first time we had a channeling session I wore heels and a skirt and, you know, I thought I was going to church. So you can imagine, if you have got a little time to study him, how he would appear dressed up in a business suit with heels on, which he has never walked in in his life.

But I guess the point that I want to tell you is that it is really difficult to talk to people — and perhaps someday I will get to do that with you, and understanding that you have gotten to meet Ramtha and know his mind and know his love and know his power — and how to understand that I am not him, and though I am working diligently on it, that we are two separate beings and that when you talk to me in this body, you are talking to me and not him. And sometimes over the past decade or so, that has been a great challenge to me in the public media because people don't understand how it is possible that a human being can be endowed with a divine mind and yet be separate from it.

So I wanted you to know that although you see Ramtha out here in my body, it is my body, but he doesn't look anything like this. But his appearance in the body doesn't lessen the magnitude of who and what he is. And you should also know that when we do talk, when you start asking me about things that he said, I may not have a clue about what you are talking about because when I leave my body in a few minutes, I am gone to a whole other time and another place that I don't have cognizant memory of. And however long he spends with you today, to me that will maybe be about five minutes or three minutes, and when I come back to my body, this whole time of this whole day has passed and I wasn't a part of it. And I didn't hear what he said to you and I don't know what he did out here. When I come back, my body is exhausted and it is hard to get up the stairs sometimes to change to make myself more presentable for what the day is bringing me, or what is left of the day.

You should also understand as beginning students, one thing that became really obvious over the years, that he has shown me a lot of wonderful things that I suppose people who have never gotten to see them couldn't even dream of in their wildest dreams. And I have seen the twenty-third universe and I have met extraordinary beings and I have seen life come and go. I have watched generations be born and live and pass in a matter of moments. I have been exposed to historical events to help me to understand better what it was I needed to know. I have been allowed to walk beside my body in other lifetimes and watch how I was and who I was, and I have been allowed to see the other side of death. So these are cherished and privileged opportunities that somewhere in my life I earned the right to have them in my life. To speak of them to other people is, in a way, disenchanting because it is difficult to convey to people who have never been to those places what it is. And I try my best as a storyteller to tell them and still fall short of it.

But I know that the reason that he works with his students the way that he does is because also Ramtha never wants to overshadow any of you. In other words, his whole point of focus is to come here and to teach you to be extraordinary; he already is. And it is not about him producing phenomena. If he told you he was going to send you runners, you are going to get them big time. It is not about him doing tricks in front of you; that is not what he is. Those are tools of an avatar that is still a guru that needs to be worshiped, and that is not the case with him.

So what will happen is he will teach you and cultivate you and allow you to create the phenomenon, and you will be able to do that. And then one day when you are able to manifest on cue and you are able to leave your body and you are able to love, when it is to the human interest impossible to do that, one day he will walk right out here in your life because you are ready to share what he is. And what he is is simply what you are going to become. And until then he is diligent, patient, all-knowing, and all-understanding of everything that we need to know in order to learn to be that.

And the one thing I can say to you is that if you are interested in what you have heard in his presentation, and you are starting to love him even though you can't see him, that is a good sign because it means that what was important in you was your soul urging you to unfold in this lifetime. And it may be against your neuronet. Your personality can argue with you and debate with you, but you are going to learn that that sort of logic is really transparent when the soul urges you onto an experience.

And I can just say that if this is what you want to do, you are going to have to exercise patience and focus and you are going to have to do the work. And the work in the beginning is very hard. But if you have the tenacity to stay with it, then one day I can tell you that this teacher is going to turn you inside out. And one day you will be able to do all the remarkable things that in myth and legend that the masters that you have heard of have the capacity to do. You will be able to do them because that is the journey. And ultimately that ability is singularly the reality of a God awakening in human form.

Now that is my journey and it has been my journey all of my life. And if it wasn't important and if it wasn't what it was, I certainly wouldn't be living in oblivion most of the year for the sake of having a few people come and have a New Age experience. This is far greater than a New Age experience. And I should also say that it is far more important than the ability to meditate or the ability to do yoga. It is about changing consciousness all through our lives on every point and to be able to unhinge and unlimit our minds so that we can be all we can be.

You should also know that what I have learned is we can only demonstrate what we are capable of demonstrating. And if you would say, well, what is blocking me from doing that, the only block that we have is our lack to surrender, our ability to surrender, our ability to allow, and our ability to support ourself even in the face of our own neurological or neuronet doubt. If you can support yourself through doubt, then you will make the breakthrough because that is the only block that stands in your way. And one day you are going to do all these things and get to see all the things that I have seen and been allowed to see.

So I just wanted to come out here and show you that I exist and that I love what I do and that I hope that you are learning from this teacher and, more importantly, I hope you continue with it.

— JZ Knight

**OUR COMMON THOUGHT
CHOOSES OUR DESTINY**

Greetings, my beloved masters, and high holidays to you. I am so happy to be with you. Let's have a drink.

O my beloved God,
I am alive,
I am awakening,
I am aware,
and I am becoming.
Of this I celebrate,
for nevermore
shall I live a life
unconsciously,
and nevermore
shall I live a life
that in the light of all eternity
I am ashamed.
O my beloved God,
I celebrate my courage
of my choice.
Long live my life,
blessed be my deeds,
and blessed be my days.
From the Lord God of my being,
so be it.
To life.

Now this evening, dedicated to coming together and creating that which is termed a new year, some of you are becoming aware of the teaching that the new year already exists as does, as you have always heard, that the past, present, and future are contained in the present. You get to swing any way you want to.

With the past we have very little options of it improving our lot in life. When we delve into the past and live as creatures from the past, when we drink from the waters of familiarity, we have very little choice in changing our futures. How many of you understand that? We are going to talk about that tonight.

So the new year has really already happened because based upon your opinion, your will, your common thought is what your year is going to be. No matter what we do here tonight, unless it is common thought the will of the personality will survive it and have its way. So then we look forward, the personality looks forward to a linear year to where it can rejoice in what it created here at this time.

But the master, the child master, the infant master in you, the one that is crawling, doesn't have to wait a year to celebrate what it wants if what it wants can be embraced utterly in mind, mind being produced by consciousness in the brain, the brain producing it from the sum total of personality/body that then begins to feel the fruit of that dream, and Spirit, that whatever choice either suppresses the Spirit or makes the Spirit grow. The fruit that we create in our mind can either grow our Holy Spirit, grow our spiritual self, or it can poison it.

So it is our common thought, it is what we really are that is going to determine this year, and it is what we really are when we conclusively decide this is the way it is going to be. Then it already is, and all we are waiting for in a linear year is to experience it through the sensual body of seeing it, smelling it, holding it, tasting it, owning it, experiencing it. That is the way of the personality. The way of the Holy Spirit is that once it is conceived in the mind, it is.

Now there are a lot of you that don't manifest very well and you are always asking why, why don't you get this and why don't you get that. You are going to understand a little bit tonight because this is a wonderful night to celebrate newness. And the message tonight is what is a master. And we are going to begin that talk by first saying that what you are going to hear tonight is an uncommon study. Now if you were a common folk of a common era, such as this one, you would be doing what all common folks of a common era would be doing tonight. So this teaching isn't for them. This teaching is not for anyone that isn't really in this school, though many will hear it, because their objectives in life are not spiritual greatness.

Choosing the Spiritual Journey

When an incarnating entity has an opportunity to wander blindly through that which is termed a physical body born in alien cultures, such as humanity, drinking the wine of forgetfulness, trying to find its way through some inward ringing — some inward calling, indeed some inward drum — wanders aimlessly in the wilderness and finally finds its way to its spiritual path, that is quite a life's journey. And so not everyone wants to follow that longing, and not everyone, though there are many paths, as it is said — Most paths have dead ends to them, because talk is cheap, philosophy is cheap, and though it is needed for the art of communication, unless it is an applicable rather than an intellect it is truly and utterly meaningless.

Now you came here like blind mice through a maze, being urged by something inside of you. It is destiny that we are together here. So when you come here to see me, don't come here expecting to hear anything else other than what you are coming to school to study. You are coming here to study about the spiritual aspect of who you are and its eternal ongoingness and how do we shift gears from being a tragic, momentary, biological unit to an everlasting, unforgettable, memorable consciousness who has been so defined that that definition is not reminiscent with the body; it is reminiscent with the divine being who knows no death.

And you have come here to hear the message. And the message was and is: You are God, a divine action upon a plane of demonstration to bring forth the unknown. So here you are. You have long study at this school, always been learning about the art of becoming profoundly spiritual. That really means profoundly conscious. And profound consciousness doesn't happen in the past; it happens in the Now, and humans live in their past, thereby defying illumination. Illumination never happens in memories. It just doesn't.

Now so you have come here to school to learn the art of being spiritually aware. You have an ulterior motive; you want to go home to God. And I tell you, you only have to go out and look at the Milky Way to decide for yourself how much life you have never lived. That is all you have to do to really be humbled. And there is in God's house many mansions, but they are only prepared for one who prepares themselves for them. They are never made available to one who never makes themselves available to them.

So you are going to learn tonight sort of a common theme, that from the first manifestation of my presence here I have taught, for there is no greater truth than that. The school then is such a priceless and beautiful place because in its humble abodes it simply concentrates upon the possible illumination of you, really you, and how to definely work out that region of divine quality in you. And it is a labyrinth because your life has been one, and you are blind and you are blind intentionally.

This school must teach you in every area so that at every point we challenge that which is termed your altered ego, who is always quick to make you lazy, it is always quick to excuse your behavior, that is always quick to make you a dishonest and immoral creature, because dishonesty and immorality are the aspects of capitalism; they are the aspects of survival. Everyone is wretched for a reason. And so the personality — the altered ego, the Antichrist, the altered Christ — is one that is concerned about its own small little body, its small little concerns: what it eats, how it looks, how much it is going to be touched, where it lives, what it has, who it is with, who it is not with. Those are strong emotional/ chemical fundamental elements to humanity.

And along the way the teaching must come so as to bring a revolution in one's life, which we call change. And the revolution is that we revolt against our limitations, and that we must have enough information and enough support and indeed enough truth that we can bring about such a marshaled revolution so as to take the personality as a wild steed and to tame it so that the Holy Spirit can ride it, instead of the other way around. You see, the blind personality is like a wild horse, and it goes here and there. It is sort of a stupid creature. It will run itself to death just to get what it wants, or to run from fear it will run itself to death. In the end it dies anyway.

The human creature is the same creature. We do not want to destroy the personality in this school of mastership but we want to revolutionize it, to bring about a revolution to where the personality is exactly the mouthpiece of the Spirit and that they are not enemies, that they are one and the same entity, so that the Holy Spirit can ride the body without objection and victimization, because many of you are victims to the concept of being masters and you intentionally make yourself that. Pity, pity. You suffer so that your personality can come back and say, "Well, I am doing this to become a master, but I am really suffering." Suffering is unnecessary when you realize the rules.

Now I like, I love, I embrace, I am Ramtha. I love my personality. I have never apologized for it, nor would I trade it in for anyone else's because it took a lot of life to make it, to tame it, to humble it, to resurrect it.

In revolutionizing the altered ego into the sublime steed of the Holy Spirit takes a lot of work. And many of you are at a disadvantage. Many of you are at a greater advantage. Those that are at a disadvantage prize their image more than they do their Spirit. And you say, well, how would I know that? It is so simple. Just look at the priorities in your life and what do you live for every day, what do you think about every day, what are you scheming about every day, where is your mind every day. That tells you where it is.

Now that means your personality and altered ego is stronger than your Spirit. That is the saying that says that the Spirit is weak and the body is strong. Then there are those people who have a very strong Spirit and a very weak body. That doesn't work either. We call those people martyrs.

What we want here is a confluence of personality and Spirit, that they are the same thing. Real clear. There is no deception, there is no aggregate, there is no lack, and there is no past. There is only this present, you see what you get, and that is what it is.

Now that is what this school is about. And it is fundamentally important that you change. But I have never asked any of you to change without sufficient knowledge to be honest about so that you could have the ability to go forward into change. Change is important. Unless you do that, you will never be balanced because until you are balanced with your personality and your Spirit, that they are the same thing, you are not going to make the steps to the master.

WHAT IS A MASTER?

Now the master. Well, what is the master? The master is when the God has come forward in full flower and is the personality, and it sparkles and it is beautiful and it is without lack and indeed it is without limitation and it is clear. And it is an entity that lives in the presence, always in the presence; everything is brought to the Now. Now that is what you all came here to go to school to become, were masters. And you call yourselves masters. I call you masters, but are you? That is what you want to be. Well, that is like placing the crown and scepter upon your head, the power in your hand. That is royalty.

But what must you do to become the master? Well, you came here tonight to listen to your teacher and to join together as that which is termed a community of spiritual beings, enriched to some degree — others, more or less — to bathe in a level of energy that would allow acceptance of dreams to come forward. That is why you are here. Well, you come to the highest pinnacle in this school when you are a walking master. And a walking master means that you have passed all of the tests in learning to ride the steed and living in the present. Up until that point, you are students of the Great Work.

I have said this to you before: There are only a few of you that will ever come out of the school and will go forward with it into the Christ state, the state to where there is no more death, there is only life. There are those of you who will take and use the tools of this school to benefit and better your own nest, your own relationship, your own life. There is nothing wrong with that, because even the most meager of changes when this life is over is going to be fundamentally wonderful. But remember what I told you in the Plane of Bliss, that what if you are already dead and you are viewing this moment, and how would you live this moment?[1] That is a cardinal rule for masters. How would this moment be lived forever and ever and ever?

Breaking Free from Our Past Emotions

Now in order for you to be better manifesters, some things you should know about yourselves, and why change is so important, and why I ask you to do it and I tell you to do it, and I send you the most precarious runners. It seems like they bring total chaos to your life. I like it. I like it because chaos breaks the loop, the emotional loop. It may cause fireworks and go all different directions, but it is supposed to. That is the reason for it. It is not unlike the way nature regenerates herself by creating chaos.

So I am going to start tonight to explain to you as students, who came here wanting to be masters, how do we then dream a year into the present moment? How do we make a year happen so momentously tonight that everything else is just a natural causeway for it to happen, and then also why would some things happen and other things not happen?

Now for a better understanding how we are going to start this, let's first write on your paper what constitutes a master, what all of you to some degree are hoping to become. At least I would hope that and desire for you, of all potentials for my people, is that that would be the great desire in all of you, that it would burn as brightly in you as your past traumas seem to do on a daily basis.

Now what is a master? A master is one who leaves no footprints. Now when we think about that, what would we interpret that saying to mean? A master has no past, that is what it means, no footprints. Now I have told you often

---

1 Ramtha, *The Mystery of Birth and Death: Redefining the Self* (Yelm: JZK Publishing, a division of JZK, Inc., 2000) pp. 130-136.

that I am marching you through my footprints going forward. Well, I am, and they are all called the present. They are the same big footprint. A master cannot be a master and be involved in the past; cannot do it.

A human being is involved in the past. That means that the way we define our altered ego, which is our limited self — listen to me very carefully — the way we define ourselves as personality — I did it; you do it — is that we define ourselves in terms of our suffering, our past. That is how we define ourselves, because unless you have a past you do not have a personality, because the first question is who are you, how did you get this way, where did you come from? Who cares? Who cares? It shouldn't be important but you do it every day. It is a habit of yours. Now listen to me. The personality can't exist as a human being unless it is fundamentally built upon its past, so it thinks in terms of past and it thinks as a survivalist. It has gotten clever. It knows what to do.

Now a master — Listen to me. You know now that your body can have its own personality, and the moment that you leave this life and go look at it, you are appalled. You are appalled, that there is part of you that can't believe that you didn't know to be better. You will be appalled, you will be, because you are going to know then who you really are, and somehow it hasn't occurred to you yet that you could have influenced all of these events. But you will be appalled because you will see the action of childhood trauma, indeed you will see the action of childhood suffering. You will see the action of rejection, no love, no this, no that, the very things that you whine in your soup about every day. You will see how those were the engines to create their own dynamics almost out of control, and you will be appalled that you lived a life that was out of control.

Now that same entity that is viewing this is this great entity that is being incarnated blindly into bodies so as to be served up opportunities to which it may feast and grow big. It wants to be a big Spirit, a holy, holy, holy, powerful archangel Spirit. It wants to grow up. It doesn't want to be a cherub. It wants to have power and meaning in its kingdom. It wants to be the big boys. Your Spirit cannot grow unless it is served the opportunities of creative force. And yet the personality seems as if it cannot survive unless it survives upon its own trauma and suffering. Quite different sort of creatures.

True Masters Are True Mystics

A master is one who has methodically changed the personality so that the personality is a window that is clean of debris. And the way that we do that willfully, as students of the Great Work, we prepare our vessel for a new wine. The vessel is the mind and the body. We prepare it for a new wine. The new wine is the Holy Spirit.

Now understand that when we have arrived at a place to where the personality is so in itself a spiritual creature — and that, my friend, is what a mystic is. A true, living mystic is one whose personality is on equal ground with its Spirit; they are both integrated. There are no enemies and no shadows. They are the same creature. That is a mystic. The personality is bold, brave, clean, clear, righteous in the mirror image of its Holy Spirit. The personality has become that living mirror of the Holy Spirit. That is what we call a righteous — the right use of — incarnation. Now that is a holy being.

Now we have people in this audience that have wonderful Spirits but lousy personalities. Those are the ones we say that have good intentions but never follow through with them. We have students in here that have great personalities but have no room for their Holy Spirit. They are charismatic; they are intellectual. They can talk but they can't do. There is nothing coming through the vessel. But when we have a true mystic in the midst, a great one, a great one is so balanced that their personality is their Holy Spirit. We call that clarity.

So now let's go back to why can't we indulge ourselves in the past and be a master, because when we move to our past, when you have moved to it, you move back into an emotional body. That creates an emotional body. It is an addiction. When you move backwards, you are moving backwards for emotion's sake.

Now a master does not have a past because these are the things that don't exist in the reality of a master. A master is not dishonest. A master is not a thief. A master is not a diplomat, which means they are not a hypocrite. A master is not a liar; the truth is as it is seen. A master is not a manipulator. Write all of these down.

Master Garola, write them down. Discuss them here, because we are going to look at how these play into a little protein called peptides from the seventh seal and what they do to the body and why a past is not worth having.

Now what are all of these? Say them. A master is not what? Now a master is truth. You know, you have heard the saying that know the truth and it will set you free. That is very important. Free from what? Free from emotions. We are going to understand that in a moment. What other things are we going to know? If we are free from emotions, then we are unattached. If we are unattached, we have no past. If we have no past, we are in the present. If we are in the present, we have clarity. That is a master. Will you turn to your neighbor and explain that. Beautiful.

THE DREAMING BRAIN
AND THE QUANTUM FIELD OF POTENTIAL

Now that we have studied all of this time in school, at least the majority of you, that which is termed the actions of the brain, little by little we have layered information upon you so that you could understand the brain, the difference in brain and consciousness, to understand the dreaming brain, which is the holographic brain that is responsible to another level of teaching that you have been taught, and that is the quantum world of particles and energy. And you have been taught that. And we put them all together, and we understood that the frontal lobe had this magical influence upon energy and that it made energy behave. So well do we understand that that science is bold enough to say that when a kind person walks in the room, they take the reading of ordinary plants, and an ordinary plant will respond to a righteous person as well as will respond to a wicked person, and so that the energy coming off of them, the Observer effect in individuals, has a profound effect upon the natural world.

So now if a plant reacts, then what about the pool of energy that you live in? We learned that it isn't superstition to say visualize and what you visualize will come true. That is not — that is not — substantial learning. Substantial learning is to get into the anatomy of energy, into the anatomy of the atomic structure, into the anatomy of molecules and possibilities, and especially the anatomy of the quantum world to which allows our greatest unfoldment that says that everything that could possibly be and what we can think and what we have yet to dream all exist simultaneously for us for our taking, that all those levels of reality exist simultaneously, and we are on a path that we have chosen simply by common thought.

Now we take all potentials, quantum world, put them into energy, put them here. The dreaming brain, the holographic brain here marry the two as Observer of consciousness and energy, and whatever this thinks, this becomes. And whatever this becomes is a chosen path of potential. From the multitudinous potentials that we could have at any moment, this is the one that we choose. And we have chosen that not as an act of awareness but as an act of unawareness. Our common thought has chosen our destiny. It isn't where we would like to be. We can say, "Well, I am sort of living this life, but I wished I was a master."

Does the life of the master exist for each of you? Absolutely. Does everyone in this room walk as an unabridged Christ? Absolutely, as an ascended being triumphant over death. Is there anyone in this room that does not have that immortal line of potential around you? Everyone in this room has it, more so because you have learned about it. But why then wouldn't it make sense to say, "But if I know it is there, how come I don't elect to be that?" It is not that we wish we could be a master — it is much more than that — it is that being the master isn't our common thought. And if it were, then the life that you are now living would dramatically change to be one of no past, total clarity, unattachment, joy, and living in the present moment where the magic presence is effervescent every moment. That already exists. So why wish for it? The truth is it is not common enough for you to be. You haven't chose it. You have chose this one. Our teaching is to get you to choose that one commonly — not forcefully, not artificially, and not as a hypocrite, and not as a fanatic but as a common way of life — then that potential exists.

So now we have the brain. How do we get the brain to make that happen? Well, first we chose the brain as computer. It knows all those potentials exist; at least this one back here knows.[2] What is the job of the brain? To dream the images that bring about common reality for

_____
2 The lower cerebellum.

fruitful experience. What is the job of the personality? To be defined by the age of thirty-two a sovereign, grounded, intelligent, lawful being, and by that to be able to have the full faculty to know righteousness and unrighteousness, the personality to be able to support goals to be accomplished in life, to support physically the desire to bring them into fruition. Instead, it is all backwards. Through the dream can the brain actually dream Christ? Yes, it can.

Biochemical Effect of Consciousness in the Body

So now we have learned all of these stages. I have meticulously brought them to you, taught you, put you in the field, challenged you, put you in the labyrinth, challenged you, blindfolded you, challenged you. We blindfold you, we blindfold the personality and we are calling for a greater something to come forward. Unfortunately, too many of you are crippled when you are blindfolded, you are crippled, because you are nothing without your personality, nothing without your eyes. And yet that is what the Holy Spirit must be, that which can ride the body, not that the body makes it but that it makes the body.

So now tonight we are going to learn then more about the emotional body, its chemical analysis, and this fabulous brain, that through the will of conscious co-op — that means the co-op of mind, body, and Spirit — we elect to understand why we choose a past in deference to a future. We are going to begin then an understanding that when you learned about the brain you did a simple, simple diagram, and it always should remain simple, and we learned how to take that yellow brain[3] mass and to break it down into neurons, and that each of these neurons had a receptor site and a synaptic cleft, and we understood that in these were neurotransmitters and also other things.

---

3 The yellow brain refers to the neocortex, which is colored yellow in Ramtha's illustration of the human brain.

We learned all of that. I also taught you that whatever the brain then calculates as a dream, that it is brought forward here in the frontal lobe, that the frontal lobe then becomes law to energy but is also the law to the body.

Now there is something I want you to understand. As a spiritual being, when we have created the image in the brain we have created reality. But the personality always begs for proof. It is always waiting for it to happen. So it shows us very simply which side we are living on, doesn't it? If we are a spiritual person, it already is. If we are a physical person, it hasn't happened yet. Simple?

Now all of the information from this picture brought together by these neurons in a neuronet fashion a hologram, and that hologram, as you learned then, was carried through this door, through here, approved by the subconscious or the God within, and then sent on down to the body, but first it happened up here.[4] So what does the body do? It consciously and chemically reacts to the picture. How many of you are you still with me? Now then that information was sent on and the body responded. But primary reality happens here, right here.[5] It is primary reality. Physical reality is secondary.

Now emotions. The brain, though it works off of the neurotransmitters — a few of them that I taught you about — it also contains within it all of that which is termed the information molecules that the body has. In other words, the word peptide is important because it has also been linked as hormones, but peptides are amino acids. They are created by that which is termed the DNA when it replicates itself through a copy called RNA, causes the cells to create all of these amino acids that are very important for distribution around the body. This is the chemical response that you get. The brain, now you should begin to understand, contains every peptide/amino acid that the body does. Whether it is in the gut, whether it is in the

4 In the brain.
5 Ibid.

adrenals, whether it is in the pancreas, it is also manufactured in the brain.

So let's pause here for a moment. Peptides are amino acids. That is what you are taking in those little blue capsules.[6] And you are taking them through a blue light, even more marvelous. Why are they so fantastic? Because these are information substances. They work on receptor sites. And you have all of these receptor sites available to all of these amino acids that literally turn you on or off.

So now if the brain contains within it all of the amino acids, the peptides, that the body uses to create emotion — are you with me; not only emotion but, remember, growth, feeling, emotion — what the brain gives the body are orders for the body to respond. Got that? What it means is that the whole body is actually living in the brain itself. So the human body is duplicated emotionally in the brain before it is ever sent to the body.

Now what this means is, for example, the hypothalamus — the hippopotamus of the brain, right here — as you have learned is responsible for the lying down of long-term memory. How many of you remember that? Raise your hands. The hypothalamus is there, is actually the keeper of past records. Let's look at it that way. Now these past records, as it were, are also stored in that which is termed peptide/amino acid hormones. That is how they are stored. Every memory is chemical and it is stored in the brain as chemicals.

Now when we have a past and we keep revisiting it, we keep wearing the past in our brain, which subsequently is passed to our bodies. Here is an example. Now the hypothalamus, its neurons that contain these peptides, dips right into that which is termed the pituitary. That means that the hypothalamus in regenerating its memory sends to the pituitary gland the information of that memory.

Now, remember, the pituitary gland is the master gland in the body. It is the great seventh seal, "Thy will be done."

6 Dietary supplements energized with a blue laser.

That memory given to the pituitary gland, the pituitary gland then approves that memory — remember, this is all chemical substance — by then sending out information into the bloodstream of the body, whose receptor sites — The chemical that emerges from the pituitary is also amino acids in the form of a hormone, as the pituitary contains all of these in hormone form. Remember, the pituitary also contains the death hormone.

Well, the long-term memory chemically reaches into the pituitary. The pituitary sends amino acids into the bloodstream that reach the adrenals. The adrenals immediately start pumping into that which is termed the bloodstream what? Steroids. Why? Because steroids the body creates because the body is in stress. Steroids help soothe the body and heal the body. Very important. They come on the heels of stress. This is an emotional feeling. It is a high. Now that emotional feeling, a relief from stress, then when the person gets all of that dumped into their body they become addicted to the depression that brings on the steroids into their body. Turn to your neighbor and tell them what I just said.

Now let's go on. Steroids in the bloodstream are a soothing agent. They are a healing agent; they are a high. Now what becomes the dilemma here is because that feels so good — it is sort of like forgiveness, "I feel better" — how many times do you have to talk about your past to someone only to say, "Gosh, I feel so much better now"? You keep the past around because it feels good to suffer. That is the way it is.

Now feel good to suffer; so what happens is as soon as that bliss wears off, you pull out the memory again. You pull the memory out. How do we do that? We go back to people, places, things, times, and events, and we go looking for redemption. Don't you hear what I am saying? You want to be troubled so you can be redeemed because you need to feel good. You are addicted to feeling good. This is the key to drug addiction — it is the key to alcoholism; it is the key to smoking too much marijuana — because you cannot feel good on your own. You are addicted to a chemical reaction, so you look for suffering so that you can be redeemed so that you could feel good. That is what it is all about.

Now these are people who cling to the past. Now what do they cling to? These are the things they cling to: this, this, this, this, this, this.[7] I can go on: victims, woe-is-me, sexuality, justness, getting back at someone, undermining. It is all here. This is only a small shopping list. People hold onto these things, and that is what a past is all about. That is what the hypothalamus is all about.

Chronic Depression

Now here is the difficulty. When you overtax that which is termed your adrenals and you keep pouring that steroid into that bloodstream over and over, you get so much of it you become toxic with it. This then is called chronic depression. Now it is not the depression we talked about when we are talking about removing ourselves and going in and not being a part of that which is termed the activity of the personality. We are talking about chronic depression, body/mind depression. So much that we are filled with steroids, that they literally begin to crowd all the receptor sites. When they do, they block out all other vital nutrients, as well as amino acids, as well as other messengers from the brain. They crowd them all out. And what begins to happen, we have receptor sites that used to facilitate calcium are now changing over to receptor sites that facilitate steroids. How many of you begin to see the picture? You are? So it becomes an addiction. People are addicted to their past. Everybody in the world is addicted to their past. It is everywhere around you.

---

7 The list of attitudes on the board: a master is not dishonest, a thief, a diplomat, a hypocrite, a liar, a manipulator.

So if this then is just a simple, simple diagram, and we are talking about it, this one chemical description of memory, hypothalamus pulling that chemical code into the pituitary, who then in turn as master gland elicits the information for the entire body — You see, the hypothalamus is a part of the limbic system. It is a part of the emotional brain. It is a part of it because the past is an emotional thing. And when we activate it, when we activate the past, we are activating emotions in the body needlessly, that then we begin to see then after a while why the pituitary issues a death hormone, because after a while the body is walking dead. It is nothing but a bag of emotional chemicals and its days are numbered. This pituitary gland as master gland of the body works in harmony with that which is termed the Spirit's soul, who begins to see that there is nothing but a suppression of spirituality taking place here for the sake of emotional addiction.

So how many other long-term memories, what other things do you have, what other issues, where are you grounded, what are you anchored in? Every hit you have in the past has got those little peptides, those amino acids, stuck to them and they are destructive. And they are calling upon continuously an emotional drain of the body itself.

Now when we talk about that in context of the first three seals,[8] we begin to understand how this works really beautifully, how that we choose to operate out of these[9] because that is where our memory is. And every time we do, we are draining the life force of the body out for an emotional high. We are actually killing the body instead of preserving it.

So what happens then? You are looking for

8 The seals are powerful energy centers connected to important glands and organs in the body that facilitate seven major and distinct levels of consciousness. The first three seals are the centers commonly at play in all of the complexities of the human drama. The first seal manifests as sexuality, the second seal as pain and suffering, and the third as power and manipulation.
9 The first three seals.

redemption. Who is going to redeem you? I will tell you something. You will never, ever find your redeemer until you find it in you. You know why? Because who has to take a stand? When are you going to say, "I have stressed myself out. I am an emotional wreck over a memory. I can't even see this present moment because all I think about is my past. I am hungry — I am hungry — for someone's sympathy. I have got to have it today. I have got to have someone's attention today. I am going to do something stupid. I am going to throw a fit. I am going to fling myself off the building. I am going to do something bizarre to get someone's attention." Why do you need someone's attention? So you can have redemption. Why do you want redemption? So that you will feel good for a while. How many of you understand that?

The past is addictive. It is not only addictive spiritually, it is addictive biochemically, indeed it is addictive personality. It is your personality. Why would you want to give up your lifestyle? If you are not going to change that, what makes you think you are going to change your emotional body? You feed off of your emotions. How many of you understand that?

Now are there other things involved? Mostly the adrenals. The sex steroids — we are talking about different ones here — those are powerful and have their own thrust. Those are also the same, that you have got to have it, you have got to have the release. You have got to have the ecstasy. You have got to have the feeling. You have got to, you have got to, you have got to. We are all talking about a bag of chemicals here that you have chosen to live your life for rather than in the light of all eternity.

Primary Reality Happens First in the Brain

Now here is my point I want to teach you about. The brain — the brain — contains every amino acid, every message, everything that the body has but more, which means what I want to tell you is this, is that what is the brain doing then? Why does the brain need adrenal steroids? "I thought they would come out of the adrenals." Is it really possible that the brain creates its own steroids? Absolutely. Does the brain create its own morphine? Absolutely. Does the brain create its own wine? Absolutely. Does the brain create its own ecstasy? Absolutely — and I am not talking about the drug Ecstasy — meaning can the brain create or re-create any substance in the world? Absolutely.

So now wake up. This is a biggie. Why would the brain have steroids in it? They are basically body entities. You know, here is the reason. We will go back to the frontal lobe. When we deliver a picture here to the frontal lobe, be that picture the past, the present, or the future — don't go to sleep — whatever we present here, the frontal cortex is bathing in neurons that contain all of the amino acids in every form. What does that mean? That means that — See this place here where we have always focused from?[10] Right behind it, it is as if there are — every nerve ending in the entire body is sitting there and they all contain within them the whole body. The whole body is sitting as negative to the frontal lobe, and whatever picture appears there holographically then automatically turns them on.

That means why does visualization — and I mean visualization, like focusing on your card,[11] focusing on your List — why is it so important? Because that is primary

---

10 The frontal lobe.
11 Discipline of Fieldwork^{SM}. See glossary.

49

consciousness and the first reality. Why would I say that? Unless you are healed in your brain, your leg will never be healed. And the idea is that if this brain contains all of the essential amino acids, all of the peptides, everything that makes up a body, it means it has got the adrenals in its brain, it has got everything there, that whatever we put in our brain we actually effect in the brain and the brain makes a copy of it chemically. Are you with me?

If you visualize that you are well, contraire to that you are not, because health is its own issue of redemption, but if we visualize, finally get with it and say, no, you are going to get well, and you put the picture there, and you are all behind yourself — your body is behind you, your personality is behind you, your brain is working, you are doing it, you are at one with self — and you put the picture there of your wellness with that much unifying focus, then in your brain you have made the marvelous healing already because you change the structure of the cells that are duplicated in the body. What we heal in the brain we neurologically and neurochemically heal in the body. If you don't heal it in the brain, you are never going to heal it in the body.

So we must make then the duplicate; we must make the voodoo doll. We must make the ghost of ourself appear so completely and to focus on it so completely in a dimension that we cause the brain itself to actually push all of the buttons and get all of the chemicals ready that make it happen in the body. We must first dream it in primary reality, even chemically, before chemically it can become so biophysically. And I don't care what it is. I don't care what it is.

Remember I told you at the beginning of this talk that all realities exist simultaneously. You are not doomed to your DNA — nor are you doomed to that which is termed your class, your culture — you are not doomed to heredity unless you approve to be so. What we can do with our brain is unfathomable. We only must have respect for the common thought of will. When we have that, we do the marvelous because whatsoever sits in that frontal lobe, it is primary reality. It is going to affect the body, and it is an emotional criteria as well as reality itself. You can heal anything. Put it there. That is why when you go out on the field and you are focusing on that card and suddenly the card in its reality is the only thing that exists — not the fence, not what time it is, not how long you have been out there, not that you must find your card, but suddenly nothing exists except the card — that is why you find the card, because you are imprinted to find it. It finally was truth without ulterior motive.

How many of you are you beginning to understand? You do? How many of you understand emotional redemption? How many of you understand the habit of it?

Now I can talk for a long time on the subject about all of the attitudes and their bodily effect, because it is all chemical, and how becoming chemically burdened by the past is such a monstrous, blinding life. But it is induced every day by every one of you and for the silliest of reasons. We are going to go to some highlights of this.

Dishonesty

What is dishonesty? Well, dishonesty is a rather relative term now, isn't it, but let us look at it from that which is termed a master's insight. First we must remember that a master does not communicate to great lengths with common mind. They don't. They have very little in common with you because you are not at a place to have that sort of mind exchange. So a master would not have to be ever dishonest with you. They just not are in your life.

So why do you keep people in your life that you have to be dishonest with? Why do you need dishonesty? Isn't that a great question? Perhaps you have never thought of it that way. Why do you need dishonesty? Well, dishonesty, dishonest, means that you know better, and knowing better is a past memory. And if you perpetrate a dishonesty in any way in your life, then you are perpetrating the past, which is connected from the hypothalamus into the pituitary that releases it emotionally in the body.

Why do you like being dishonest? Because it is a game you play. Being dishonest allows you to be powerful but at the same time fearful, because you may get caught. That is the fear aspect. The power aspect is that you think you are pulling something over on someone, and that is all chemical. It is an elated, powerful, addictive place.

So people are dishonest because of the chemical reaction it gives them. People go out and are very stupid. They walk precipices just for the thrill of nearly dying. The thrill of nearly dying is walking the razor's edge and creating fear, all for chemical release. What is it to almost die and defeat death but risk your life in stupidity and ignorance? It is for chemicals, isn't it? No master lives that way, no master does, only a fool. Why? Because a master does not need to create an emotional addiction to fear and dishonesty. Dishonesty means he would have to be linked to his past, or her past, in order to perpetrate dishonesty. Why wouldn't a master want to be dishonest? Because it links them to their past, and if they are in the past, they are out of the present and the present is where they find their power, not in the past.

So I would say to you, what master would ever think you were worth being dishonest for? None. You are not worth any of that. So why are they so elusive in your life? Because you are not worthy of their presence, and they would rather not have you in their life than have you in their life. They are being honest. You are trouble. You have not the same mind. You thrive off of dishonesty. They are free with truth because they have severed all of the past's connections to people, places, things, times, and events.

Do you know what happens when you do that? You have a sense of freedom. The pituitary gland in the brain no longer emits informational peptides to cause emotional reaction in the body. You say, well, that seems rather a blandish sort of life. No. In the place of that, the pituitary lives, secretes a hormone that is the immortal hormone. I mean immortal. And where we get peace and joy is that we are free in truth. What are we seeking freedom from? What is truth? The freedom from the past, everything that binds us to ignorance, stupidity, to act less than the grace of our divine self, and to tie us in for some sort of game that only gives us emotional pleasure until we dry up and have no more emotions to give. Then we are done for, another miserable, wretched life.

Listen. Dishonesty is manipulation and manipulation is self-serving. How is it self-serving? It is chemically self-serving. Walking the edge, almost getting caught, and manipulation, they are all emotional.

Stealing from Others

Now a thief. A master would never take from someone what is not theirs. Why would they ever need to do that? No one in the world has anything that a master wants that they couldn't create themselves. Remember the story about the student who sits outside the gates of the great city, and he is looking at everyone who comes in and out to see if he has missed anything?[12] And he sits there and sits there and sits there and checks all of those fabulous caravans, all of those flotillas coming in and all of those exotic people and all of those wonderful smells, and sits there like a beggar, and every once in a while they give him a few alms. He is really watching to see if he has missed anything. Finally it occurs to him after many years he hasn't missed anything. When he realized that, he didn't have a past; he left this plane. In the middle of a poppy field, he left this plane. No footprints. They stopped. He went.

12 *Selected Stories III.* Tape 033 ed. (Yelm: Ramtha Dialogues, 1989), Story II: *Leaving No Footprints.*

Now when you steal something from someone, you are being dishonest. A thief is really one who will not bend their back or their mind for their own manifestation and really are predators that prey upon others. And they get it through different ways. They take what they have not created. That is a thief. They are emotionally wounded because they are lazy. Taking is the way that they create, not creating. A master doesn't have to take anything and wouldn't take anything because there is nothing that you have that they cannot manifest because, you see, they have already learned the magical secret that consciousness and energy creates reality and it is better to create it on their own than to take it from another. That is the challenge in life.

You see, that is the difference between living as a personality and living to feed the cherub to become an archangel. We make our Holy Spirit strong by providing challenges and lacks that it may be bountiful and triumphant in. I would rather you have nothing, starve, before you took even a sweet-cake from someone else that wasn't yours, because I would rather see you pit a challenge to your Holy Spirit. You see, we are here not to take handouts; we are here to make it happen. That is why you are in this school.

Now a master doesn't take anything, and would never, until he could manifest it himself. That is what makes us powerful. That is what makes us powerful. It is sort of like going out in the field and lifting your blinders and looking at two or three cards just for the sake of finding your card; you have missed the purpose of the training. The training is to bring about and grow the Holy Spirit and let it define the personality, that you can do anything. You walk off that field, you can heal the sick and raise the dead. But it is not going to work if you only go out in the field and peek and cheat, which some of you do regularly. You have missed the point of the training.

And the same is in life. You don't take anything from

anyone that doesn't belong to you. And the challenge is not what you can receive but what you can create. That is the challenge. That is when you may have to pull in your belt. But I would never feel sorry for one who takes a stand on their own life. I never feel sorry for someone who lost everything, who is having to cinch in their belt buckle and it says "beyond hungry" over here. I would never feel sorry for them — why would you? — because I know they are making a stand. They are taking a stand against their body and their emotions and their needs and putting it right into the Holy Spirit. And they are going to make this happen, and that is the most important thing to them. Getting it through other sources is not the answer. It is making God make it. Now that is my kind of master. That is my kind of master, can take it right to the edge and jump off with it. That is a personality that will become God.

The Lie behind Diplomacy

You steal, you are no master. You are dishonest, you are no master. You are emotionally tied into the thrill of what it gives you. You are addicted to redemption. A diplomat, you know what a diplomat is? A clever liar, a clever liar. They are always gray. They are the kind of people that move like flotsam and jetsam on the water, but they are not the movement; they are simply what floats on it.

You have to understand, you ever get to talk to a master — and some of you do every time you see me — that I am never going to always answer your questions or do what you ask. And why wouldn't I answer all of your questions? You don't have the mind to understand the answer. You don't have what it takes to make it happen. Why should I help you? I know your intent before you even open your mouth.

Being a master doesn't mean that you have to accompany someone and be diplomatic to them. Being a master says I am here because I want to be here. And it doesn't mean that you have to beat around the bush and tell stories and fibs and all of that. You can enjoy perhaps the first and most meaningful conversation of your life when you tell the truth and you are honest in the moment. Being honest isn't brutal. It is a breath of fresh air.

Don't ask someone how they feel if you don't want to hear the answer. Don't ask them how they feel. Don't say "I understand" all along the way every time they open their mouth. Don't do that, because maybe you don't understand. Don't sympathize with thieves. Don't sympathize with dishonest people. Don't sympathize with victims who prey off of emotion. Why would you want to do that? Kindness is the hallmark of God, but to get down and to wallow in it is not what a master is.

You learn the truth about someone and that is what it must be. To delusionalize yourself is only to trap yourself in an emotional delusion, and that we do not want. We become great in this school for the sake of the world, but we must be that in spite of the world in order to arrive at that most prestigious of places, that rare academy and fraternity which only a few beings have even been able to accomplish. You have the opportunity to do it today.

But I tell you, it is so hard for you to tell the truth because most of you don't know what it is. You know why you don't know the truth? I will tell you why you don't know the truth. You can't tell anyone the truth because you are emotionally addicted to redemption. How could you tell anyone the truth? How do you know? You haven't mastered your own redemption. How can you say to someone "I understand"? You don't understand because you are in just as much a game as they are. You toy with the past. You set your hook in the waters of the past. You are there because you want to be. Don't tell anyone you understand, because you don't know what the truth is, because the truth is very freeing and if you knew it, you wouldn't tarry where you are at, nor would you tarry in your libelous — libelous, meaning the body will sue you for life — your libelous injunction of truth in the place of emotional gratification. You know why? Because you want something from someone. What kind of conversation are you going to have if you don't feel pity and sympathy and if they don't glorify you or aggrandize you? What kind of conversation do you want? Somebody to listen to you.

What if you understood the truth and realized that no matter what I tell this person, they are never going to listen to me because all I am giving them is temporary redemption, a Ramtha fix, and they are going to go back home and it is going to wear off, and they are going to need it again to be relieved of what they themselves can't even begin to fathom, is a truth that is closer than the air in their lungs.

We are not without the faculty to master this world and the afterlife. It is just you are too damned lazy, and you are afraid you are going to offend someone. And really the person you are going to offend is you, because you have never gotten to the truth of you. You have never been honest creatures. You have never simply done anything for the sake of truth. It has always had an ulterior motive behind it. You don't know what love is because you don't know what truth is yet. And, you see, love is that which alleviates emotional addiction for redemption.

And where do we get love? We first seek it in others. But we shall never find it in others until we have loved ourself enough to understand that we are on a reincarnation roller coaster and that we are addicted to our moods and that we are addicted to our heights and our depression; we are addicted to our victimization. No one will ever save us. You would think, "Where are these masters that couldn't have saved me? For ten and a half million years I have been living the same lie. Why didn't someone tell me so?" We have.

And you come down here with great intentions, and you get in that body and you go to town. You spill your seed as if it will never stop, and it will. It will stop. You lie. You are dishonest. You are a diplomat. You don't even know who you are. You do everything for emotions and moods. You think joy is a state of redemption. But I tell you, joy is when we are detached emotionally because then the pituitary creates those great hormones that bring about bliss.

The Truth Releases Our Guilt

Is it possible for the body's organism to live in bliss? Yes, and the emotional experience is called truth. We do not know how else to tell you that truth is love. You think "love" because it is sexual, "I love this person because I feel so good intercoursing with them." You think that is love. No, that is chemicals. Don't you know everything else is?

But what of the great love? Love is a hormone carried by the pituitary that is the great seventh seal, that when we are no longer dishonest, no longer thieves, no longer diplomats, no longer manipulators, no longer liars, no longer victims, no longer fools, no longer drug addicts — And, by the way, don't any of you ever speak for me. I do not approve of Ecstasy or any hallucinogenic that you take. You are delusional. When I tell you you are a master and that you are self-made and that you have every chemical in your brain, I am telling you that the divine is not crippled. The divine has a brain, that it can heal an entire body by re-creating it. If you are a master, you don't need to be out of your gourd. You only need to be truth. That is all you need. And when you are clear, you won't have emotions running, you won't have to hide, you won't have to be freaked out. What do you think you are going to see when you do all of this, other dimensions? How in the world can you see other dimensions when you can't even see yourself? You are blind. You are emotionally blind.

Now a master finds that the art of forgiveness — And one great thing that the church did do was to provide an entity to where one could commit the blunders of oneself, to pay penance for it, that one could have a confessor to where they could confess all of this. That is a very ennobling thing. Unfortunately, they are not divine men.

The way that you pull the anchor out of the past of people, places, things, times, and events is you get rid of everything that haunts you, hurts you, makes you feel guilty, that you have hidden, that you have done. You have to address it because you are going to address it at the light.[13] When you do and come clean, you are pulling yourself out of the roots of the past. You are pulling them up. Who in this world is worth holding onto deception for? Who? Are they going to die for you? There is no one in this room going to die for you, no one. You think your drug dealers will die for you? No one is going to die for you. Then why would you want to live for them? Why?

What have you done that is so awful that you keep it buried and covered up, except to those who can see it? Why don't you uncover it and you look at it, and why don't you get rid of it without emotion? Why don't you confess it without emotion? Who cares if they don't like you any longer? You are not doing it for them. You are doing it for you.

The journey is an alone journey. It is not a social-conscious journey. Look at our numbers that are gathered here tonight. I am an awesome being, prophesied long ago, and the numbers are small. But you are the ones who made it here. Look at you.

Who do you want to live for out there? You made the journey to come here. What would keep you from going on? Truth is then that clean and pristine mirror. You know why? Think of it this way. When we redeem ourselves, we are pulled out of the past and we are buoyantly in the present. And there is no memory that keeps coming forward that chemically depresses the body or subjugates it to need or addiction.

---

13 The light or life review after death.

You say, "Well, then how can a misdeed that I did to someone and they didn't know about it — better that I didn't tell them." I will tell you why. It isn't important that you didn't tell them. It is important that you didn't tell them, meaning you confronted it yourself. It was a dishonest act.

What is it about guilt? Guilt holds us to the past and makes us feel bad, that we look at our life for redemption only to find redemption and then to use the guilt to feel bad so we can be redeemed again. Guilt is self-serving. It is. Victims are self-serving. When you hide things in the past, you are not clean. You are a past person. I don't care how spiritual you can talk it. If you can't walk it, you are not it. The truth liberates us from the past — those dark secrets, those misdeeds, those lies, those mistrusts, those manipulations — they liberate you from the past and make you clean in here. You don't know it tonight, but when you thrive off of secrets, you chemically damage your body. Your body is always in stress. Don't you know cancer wouldn't exist if there wasn't the past? Cancer wouldn't exist if there wasn't guilt and then self-hatred? We hate other people because they are a reflection of what we are most ashamed of in ourselves. Do you understand that?

The Morality of a Master

Now a master isn't any of those.[14] Do you know why? Because the glory of God is found in the present, not in the past. And the glory of God shines through us when we live in this moment. And in our freedom we have no obstruction to our dreams; we have no ulterior motive. Our dream doesn't have to go through our guilt and then be filtered as something else at the other end. Our desire for healing is not curved by our shame. Shame can prevent a healing. Guilt can prevent a healing. Lying, dishonesty, all that prevents healing. We have nothing to then prevent our

14 Dishonesty, theft, diplomacy, hypocrisy, deception, manipulation, etc.

healing because we are clear. And what then as masters can we not do? We have nothing standing in our way. Masters like to keep the company of masters. A person isn't beautiful unless they are beautiful spiritually.

What does this do? How do we then make that the perfect mystic? When we have the great personality that matches the great Spirit. The journey allows us to be so stalwart in our desire to be present, that when we have pulled anchor from the past we have changed the personality. The personality becomes changed. Who are you on the other side if you have no past? What if you had amnesia? Would you still love those people that you thought you loved? I daresay you wouldn't, because it is a chemical bond. If you had amnesia and forgot you had any problems, would you be healthy? I daresay you would be. Who would you be beholden to if you had amnesia? No one. Everyone would be trying to find you but you wouldn't know that you were trying to be found. How many of you understand that? That is a blessed way to be.

But then when we do this work, when we understand our artificial need for an artificial physical high and we understand it in very mature terms, we start to create a personality that can match marvelously with the Holy Spirit. Now we have the great union. We do have the Christ and the bridegroom. Now the husbandman and the bridegroom, we have them together now, perfect unity, perfect intercourse. Now we have the mystic. Now we have the master. Now we really have something quite beautiful and rare. We create the holy personality by getting rid of all of those things.

So is a master then a moralist? To the highest degree. Is a master impeccable? To the highest degree. Does a master live for anyone? No one but God. Is a master strong? Stronger than the foundations of the world.

Now that is what this school is endeavoring to teach you. And I can say these words from here to the next high holidays, and there are some of you who will never hear me because your modus operandi is about your body, your personality, and your addiction to suffering, pain, abuse, and how well it has served you, and you will never hear the message. You will covet your wrongs. You will covet your lies. You will covet that which is termed your infidelities. You will covet and, like nasty little riches, hold them in a secret place and you won't let go of them because they serve you. They serve to punish you and to reward you. You will never hear the message. And only a few will hear and only a few will change.

WHY DO MASTERS LIVE FOREVER?

So then what happens when you get clear? Everything is possible. Why would a master go back to people, places, things, times, and events if he is on the verge of going on the other side of Point Zero? He wouldn't. Is the brain then capable of substantiating and creating a consciousness to where is it possible that this consciousness can make a brain that is so superior? Is it possible that the brain could become the brain of Christ? Is it possible? Yes. Does the brain have the ability to become God? Yes, it is made to do that. If it is then and we have reached a level of proportion to where our personality is so for this dynamic, this dynamic union and agreement, is it possible then that our mind could be the mind of God? Yes.

And what does that mean then? That means then that whatsoever, we who are free — we who are free of our torments, our sufferings, our anguishes, our bitternesses, our disappointments — we who are free of the past have the marvelous liberty of being able to dream a dream and, no matter how fantastic, have a brain that is so ready on the epitome of opportunisticness to be able to replicate that dream and become it physically. We have a brain, that if we dream in utter freedom that we have deserved in truth, that we could bring our body to immortality, that our body should never die and that we should never age, that if we dreamed such a dream, our brain is capable of matching that dream chemically. And the pituitary, who is the master seventh seal, has the ability to take this body into infinity. It is encoded.

If there are twenty-two or twenty amino acids — I tell you, there are more than that; they have just never been discovered, and these important chemicals have already encoded in them the highest potential you could ever be. How do masters live forever? And they do, because when they are free, they get to dream the dream of foreverness and there is nothing that clouds. There is no regret, there is no resentment, there is no sadness, there is no anguish, there is no victim. There is nothing that that dream has to bypass. That brain imprints that dream and this body becomes it. At any level we can transcend. Then we have done the Great Work. Then we have come here, we have created, we have overcome and overcome to become. And we leave as we came as wind on the water, integrated into clay — we take the clay and transform it into dust on the water — and we leave no footprints, no body, no grave. We are gone.

The brain has the same capacity to create immortality, to create wellness, to create and duplicate itself many times. You can do anything. You are not limited, nor are you limited biochemically. You are only limited by your preference of consciousness, your preference of mind, your preference of personality. Whose side are you on? Are you on the side of the body or are you on the side of the Spirit? Isn't it time if you are in this school to not be afraid to make the radical changes in your life that liberate you, that liberate you from deception? A deception, though may be glamorous and mysterious and allows you to walk on the edge and to be clever, in the end will always be found out, only to be appalled at the light in reviewing your life and appalled that you wasted this life being a fool.

You haven't missed anything except truth. You go out in the world and have a good time. What is a good time? It is emotions. But you will miss truth. Remember that. Turn to your neighbor and explain what you have learned tonight. How many of you have learned so far tonight? You have? Are you getting a closer understanding of what it takes to be a master? Are you getting an understanding of why change is important?

Why Don't We Manifest Our Wishes?

So why hasn't everything manifested that you wanted? Because there are other things that were more important to it: unworthiness, failure. Failure is always an excellent topic because people love failure and they love to feel like failures, because in feeling like that, they never have to be expected to go on and accomplish. It is easy to be a failure because you never accomplish anything but being a failure. So it sort of saves you from risking yourself, I suppose.

You don't get many things because of the agreement you have with your personality. People who live in the past never really get the things they wish for, because what is common thought to them is what they are addicted to mentally. It makes up their personality. You can't get from the Spirit, who is less than the personality, what does not serve the personality. Did you know that? And you have an unspoken law about your personality. Your personality is made up of all of the variables of these things chemically. It is all based in chemicals. You have laws that operate your personality for chemical expression, and some of the things that you wish for would violate those laws. You are not really ready to give them up. You are not really ready to give them up. There are certain things that you ask for that would violate many of your chemical laws, so they are less spiritually; the more powerful personality will be always dominant in that factor. So you would say, "Well, aren't we, alas, then as you have said, we can have anything that is around us?" Of course, but what usually is common thought is our common law. And if the law of our personality is made up in thick concentration upon these things that keep us emotionally fed, then our common law is what is going to take precedence over a wish.

In order for dynamic reality to happen it must be common thought. It must be a law, that we can then ascertain from that is that we are not going to enter the kingdom of heaven as a whining victim. So either we enjoy the pursuit of redemption, which is a chemical high — a downer, a high, a downer, a high, touchy-feely, huggy, all of that — either we go for that or we go for the kingdom of heaven.

What does it mean to say the kingdom of heaven? "I choose to be a spiritual being and I choose to ride my personality until it reflects me perfectly. I do not choose to be a body that dictates to my Spirit its whims and needs. I am diminished by such a horrible thought." How many of you understand?

So you can't have abundance if you are looking for redemption. And if you get it, you will lose it. How many of you understand? You can't have health — you can't have health — you can't have health if you have created illness, when it serves you so well. You blabbed all your life about how bad the world was and, you know, all of those chemicals served you until you became unhealthy. Unhealthiness is a state of mind. And you put so much stress into your body and preyed off of that emotion for so long that it served you, that you can't even facilitate health in your body because all of your receptor sites have turned into facilitating steroids, salt. You can't be healthy. So now what happens? Your body is going haywire. Now you finally get what you have served up all of these years. You cannot expect a miracle if being unhealthy is self-serving. How many of you understand that? Furthermore, you are not going to be happy if happy doesn't serve you. Correct? And you are never going to know the truth because you are afraid of it because it may liberate you, and who in the hell would you be then?

The War Cry of Change and Self-Conquest

You came here to be masters. Don't you know that is going to be an awfully different person than the one who walked in this door? And don't you know that it means change? And don't you know that if you are hung up on your sexuality and you are hung up on all of that — you are hung up on chemicals and you are hung up on redemption — don't you know that you are going to be a different person and that you need to be in order to become what you have come here to learn? And don't you know that all of the things that you fathom the master can be are at hand? Don't you know they are closer than the breath in your lungs? But what is it that you choose? You choose to be unchallenged.

This is going to challenge you, my beautiful people. It is no accident that the great ones are few, because you have to overcome your humanity. That is not easy because you do everything for the glory of other people. And you need them, you know? We do warrior cries in here, we do C&E®, and you get that great spiritual cry coming that releases so much emotions, puts all of that protein in the blood. Don't you know it is a life force happening? Don't you know that when you give that warrior cry you are releasing that suppressed emotion you are afraid to look at? Release is why you feel so marvelous, you feel light, because in your blood is an extraordinary amount of amino acids in the form of peptides that form proteins. These are all life-giving agents. That is why you feel so wonderful, because it is a release and it is a surrender to God.

But it takes work. How long is it going to take you to get the message? How long is it going to take you to become wealthy? When you stop depending upon woe-is-me to get an emotional charge, that is how long. When you stop feeling pity for yourself, that is how long. When you stop using other people, when you stop stealing, when you stop lying, when you stop all of those things that have given you your advantage in life, when you stop all of that and take a stand — and you know the truth about yourself, and you go digging and you get it out and you are going to manifest that — that is when it will happen. And you know when you are going to get well? When you stop feeling sorry for yourself and realize you have gotten really far in this life by being an abused child. And it is just about to get you. Enough, enough. That is a lot of change.

And you can't love people for money, though you do. It seems to be an important thing. You don't even know what it is until you know truth. Then we will talk about love. Then we will really talk about the spiritual substance that is rare and beautiful. Then we will learn what it is. Until then, you don't know what it is. Are you willing to admit that and are you willing to change? Are you willing to admit to yourself and pull out all of your dirty secrets and look at them, because you are going to have to. Either you do it now or you do it when this baby is over with, and then it is going to be appalling. And then you are going to be appalled at how many of us watched it all.

You can be free. And it is important that you do that. And there comes an extraordinary detachment in being that way. Then you are even and level, honorable, and that is a rare, rare thing in the world, my beautiful people, rare.

Are you willing to do that? Some, not all. But that is what it is going to take. And then how long does the mastery take? Not long, because like magic you will be flooded with an indescribable joy. And it is as if the world has been released from your shoulders, and it will be. And that is when you break that cycle in the body of emotional dependency. When you are free of it, you are free. Then you are totally present.

Don't go looking for trouble. Don't go looking for your past, and don't beg for it to come back into your life. If you do, you are a fool. The moment you do, you leave the present, the magical present — the magical present — this one. Why would you leave this for this?[15] None of us have ever done that. We don't have any desire to do that. Why should you? Think about it.

So tonight when you create this new year, the first thing you must do — And I know you are already a little weary, but you haven't seen me in a long time and someone needs

---

15 The present-Now for the past.

to tell you you are just a bag of chemicals, and you are going to have to get that under control before you can walk this Earth in grace. Before you create your year, you are going to have to go and dig these ugly little creatures out, and you have to blow them away tonight.[16] I mean be committed to it. It is when you take a stand and say — look around you — who do I perpetuate this life for? Look around. Who is going to throw a rock at you? Why, we are looking at a whole group of sinners here. Everybody should be stoned. Who are you hiding from? Only humans. You don't hide from the Spirit.

So find yourself. You be found, and go looking for it. Blow it all away. And you find those ugly little necromancers, and you pull them right up, and you get it on, and you address them. And you get them out and you blow them away. And you get clean. And you do that until you are shining and you feel — you feel — a state of bliss. Then in that state you put into it what you want. And in that magic presence, everything happens.

Remember what I am telling you. The brain is necessary to create reality. That is why you have it. Furthermore, the brain has everything the body has but more. It duplicates the body not only visually but chemically and electrically. Whatever you put there — whatever you put there — the brain will chemically match it. As above, so below; as within, so without. Then it becomes. There is no way it is not going to happen.

How does having a vision in your brain have anything to do with an extraordinary body? It has everything to do with it. How do we visualize the Spirit? Everything that we are not. Can the brain match that? Yes, it can.

So tonight first we are going to create the entire year. But the greatest creation that we do tonight is to unburden ourselves with the foolish masks that have kept us from walking as Gods, what we are truly meant to be, unburden our deceptions, our dishonesty, our lies, all of it, our emotional lacking, our neediness, our cleverness, all of

---

16 Using the discipline of C&E®.

those things. You blow them away and you find them. When you are free, put one clean thing in their place and create this year, and like magic it will be destiny unfolding. The moment you go into your past and pull up a long-term memory, you start the chemical reactions in the body. The moment that you create a marvelous future in the present, it starts that moment. Got it? So be it.

So now I want you to put on your blindfolds. I want you to spend some time contemplating what it is you hide and what it is that you depend upon. And you contemplate it, and as soon as you find it, I want you to engage the breath with all of your might, and I want you to blow it out and keep blowing it out until you cannot even form the thought any longer in your brain. And you find what it is that cripples you, and you heal it. And when you are ready and you feel wonderful, you create your year, but not until you have cleaned house. Got it?

P.S., I love you, or I wouldn't be here.

And what did you accomplish tonight? Did you simply hear or did you become? Did you change or avoid? Did you hear? You are divine. How can I say that in words that you can understand better than these? You are divine. It is by your own hand that your life is either the life of Christ or a pauper. It is by your own hand that you live eternally or you die. It is by your own mind what you suffer from, are free from.

You came to school to draw nearer to God and to be the master along the way. In order to become the master you have to stop being the human addicted to emotions and you have to change. That is what you came to learn. And only until you do that are you going to be able to have such a clear conscience that straightaway every thought that is common is equally matched in the twinkling of an eye by its companion energy.

This then is the consequence of the master, to be God/man or God/woman realized, but God first, above everything else. So be it.

I love you.

RAMTHA'S GLOSSARY

Analogical. Being analogical means living in the Now. It is the creative moment and is outside of time, the past, and the emotions.

Analogical mind. Analogical mind means one mind. It is the result of the alignment of primary consciousness and secondary consciousness, the Observer and the personality. The fourth, fifth, sixth, and seventh seals of the body are opened in this state of mind. The bands spin in opposite directions, like a wheel within a wheel, creating a powerful vortex that allows the thoughts held in the frontal lobe to coagulate and manifest.

Bands, the. The bands are the two sets of seven frequencies that surround the human body and hold it together. Each of the seven frequency layers of each band corresponds to the seven seals of seven levels of consciousness in the human body. The bands are the auric field that allow the processes of binary and analogical mind.

Binary mind. This term means two minds. It is the mind produced by accessing the knowledge of the human personality and the physical body without accessing our deep subconscious mind. Binary mind relies solely on the knowledge, perception, and thought processes of the neocortex and the first three seals. The fourth, fifth, sixth, and seventh seals remain closed in this state of mind.

Blue Body®. It is the body that belongs to the fourth plane of existence, the bridge consciousness, and the ultraviolet frequency band. The Blue Body® is the lord over the lightbody and the physical plane.

Blue Body® Dance. It is a discipline taught by Ramtha in which the students lift their conscious awareness to the consciousness of the fourth plane. This discipline allows the Blue Body® to be accessed and the fourth seal to be opened.

Blue Body® Healing. It is a discipline taught by Ramtha in which the students lift their conscious awareness to the consciousness of the fourth plane and the Blue Body® for the purpose of healing or changing the physical body.

Blue webs. The blue webs represent the basic structure at a subtle level of the physical body. It is the invisible skeletal structure of the physical realm vibrating at the level of ultraviolet frequency.

Body/mind consciousness. Body/mind consciousness is the consciousness that belongs to the physical plane and the human body.

Book of Life. Ramtha refers to the soul as the Book of Life, where the whole journey of involution and evolution of each individual is recorded in the form of wisdom.

C&E® = R. Consciousness and energy create the nature of reality.

C&E®. Abbreviation of Consciousness & Energy[SM]. This is the service mark of the fundamental discipline of manifestation and the raising of consciousness taught in Ramtha's School of Enlightenment. Through this discipline the students learn to create an analogical state of mind, open up their higher seals, and create reality from the Void. A Beginning C&E® Workshop is the name of the Introductory Workshop for beginning students in which they learn the fundamental concepts and disciplines of Ramtha's teachings. The teachings of the Beginning C&E® Workshop can be found in *Ramtha, A Beginner's Guide to Creating Reality,* third ed. (Yelm: JZK Publishing, a division of JZK, Inc., 2004), and in *Ramtha, Creating Personal Reality*, Tape 380 ed. (Yelm: Ramtha Dialogues, 1998).

Christwalk. The Christwalk is a discipline designed by Ramtha in which the student learns to walk very slowly being acutely aware. In this discipline the students learn to manifest, with each step they take, the mind of a Christ.

Consciousness. Consciousness is the child who was born from the Void's contemplation of itself. It is the essence and fabric of all being. Everything that exists originated in consciousness and manifested outwardly through its handmaiden energy. A stream of consciousness refers to the continuum of the mind of God.

Consciousness and energy. Consciousness and energy are the dynamic force of creation and are inextricably combined. Everything that exists originated in consciousness and manifested through the modulation of its energy impact into mass.

Create Your DaySM. This is the service mark for a technique created by Ramtha for raising consciousness and energy and intentionally creating a constructive plan of experiences and events for the day early in the morning before the start of the day. This technique is exclusively taught at Ramtha's School of Enlightenment.

Disciplines of the Great Work. Ramtha's School of Ancient Wisdom is dedicated to the Great Work. The disciplines of the Great Work practiced in Ramtha's School of Enlightenment are all designed in their entirety by Ramtha. These practices are powerful initiations where the student has the opportunity to apply and experience firsthand the teachings of Ramtha.

Emotional body. The emotional body is the collection of past emotions, attitudes, and electrochemical patterns that make up the brain's neuronet and define the human personality of an individual. Ramtha describes it as the seduction of the unenlightened. It is the reason for cyclical reincarnation.

Emotions. An emotion is the physical, biochemical effect of an experience. Emotions belong to the past, for they are the expression of experiences that are already known and mapped in the neuropathways of the brain.

Energy. Energy is the counterpart of consciousness. All consciousness carries with it a dynamic energy impact, radiation, or natural expression of itself. Likewise, all forms of energy carry with it a consciousness that defines it.

Enlightenment. Enlightenment is the full realization of the human person, the attainment of immortality, and unlimited mind. It is the result of raising the kundalini energy sitting at the base of the spine to the seventh seal that opens the dormant parts of the brain. When the energy penetrates the lower cerebellum and the midbrain, and the subconscious mind is opened, the individual experiences a blinding flash of light called enlightenment.

Evolution. Evolution is the journey back home from the slowest levels of frequency and mass to the highest levels of consciousness and Point Zero.

FieldworkSM. FieldworkSM is one of the fundamental disciplines of Ramtha's School of Enlightenment. The students are taught to create a symbol of something they want to know and experience and draw it on a paper card. These cards are placed with the blank side facing out on the fence rails of a large field. The students blindfold themselves and focus on their symbol, allowing their body to walk freely to find their card through the application of the law of consciousness and energy and analogical mind.

Fifth plane. The fifth plane of existence is the plane of superconsciousness and x-ray frequency. It is also known as the Golden Plane or paradise.

Fifth seal. This seal is the center of our spiritual body that connects us to the fifth plane. It is associated with the thyroid gland and with speaking and living the truth without dualism.

First plane. It refers to the material or physical plane. It is the plane of the image consciousness and Hertzian frequency. It is the slowest and densest form of coagulated consciousness and energy.

First seal. The first seal is associated with the reproductive organs, sexuality, and survival.

First three seals. The first three seals are the seals of sexuality, pain and suffering, and controlling power. These are the seals commonly at play in all of the complexities of the human drama.

Fourth plane. The fourth plane of existence is the realm of the bridge consciousness and ultraviolet frequency. This plane is described as the plane of Shiva, the destroyer of the old and creator of the new. In this plane, energy is not yet split into positive and negative polarity. Any lasting changes or healing of the physical body must be changed first at the level of the fourth plane and the Blue Body®. This plane is also called the Blue Plane, or the plane of Shiva.

Fourth seal. The fourth seal is associated with unconditional love and the thymus gland. When this seal is activated, a hormone is released that maintains the body in perfect health and stops the aging process.

God. Ramtha's teachings are an exposition of the statement, "You are God." Humanity is described as the forgotten Gods, divine beings by nature who have forgotten their heritage and true identity. It is precisely this statement that represents Ramtha's challenging message to our modern age, an age riddled with religious superstition and misconceptions about the divine and the true knowledge of wisdom.

God within. It is the Observer, the great self, the primary consciousness, the Spirit, the God within the human person.

God/man. The full realization of a human being.

God/woman. The full realization of a human being.

Gods. The Gods are technologically advanced beings from other star systems who came to Earth 455,000 years ago. These Gods manipulated the human race genetically, mixing and modifying our DNA with theirs. They are responsible for the evolution of the neocortex and used the human race as a subdued work force. Evidence of these events is recorded in the Sumerian tablets and artifacts. This term is also used to describe the true identity of humanity, the forgotten Gods.

Golden body. It is the body that belongs to the fifth plane, superconsciousness, and x-ray frequency.

Great Work. The Great Work is the practical application of the knowledge of the Schools of Ancient Wisdom. It refers to the disciplines by which the human person becomes enlightened and is transmuted into an immortal, divine being.

GridSM, The. This is the service mark for a technique created by Ramtha for raising consciousness and energy and intentionally tapping into the Zero Point Energy field and the fabric of reality through a mental visualization. This technique is exclusively taught at Ramtha's School of Enlightenment.

Hierophant. A hierophant is a master teacher who is able to manifest what they teach and initiate their students into such knowledge.

Hyperconsciousness. Hyperconsciousness is the consciousness of the sixth plane and gamma ray frequency.

Infinite Unknown. It is the frequency band of the seventh plane of existence and ultraconsciousness.

Involution. Involution is the journey from Point Zero and the seventh plane to the slowest and densest levels of frequency and mass.

JZ Knight. JZ Knight is the only person appointed by Ramtha to channel him. Ramtha refers to JZ as his beloved daughter. She was Ramaya, the eldest of the children given to Ramtha during his lifetime.

Kundalini. Kundalini energy is the life force of a person that descends from the higher seals to the base of the spine at puberty. It is a large packet of energy reserved for human evolution, commonly pictured as a coiled serpent that sits at the base of the spine. This energy is different from the energy coming out of the first three seals responsible for sexuality, pain and suffering, power, and victimization. It is commonly described as the sleeping serpent or the sleeping dragon. The journey of the kundalini energy to the crown of the head is called the journey of enlightenment. This journey takes place when this serpent wakes up and starts to split and dance around the spine, ionizing the spinal fluid and changing its molecular structure. This action causes the opening of the midbrain and the door to the subconscious mind.

Life force. The life force is the Father/Mother, the Spirit, the breath of life within the person that is the platform from which the person creates its illusions, imagination, and dreams.

Life review. It is the review of the previous incarnation that occurs when the person reaches the third plane after death. The person gets the opportunity to be the Observer, the actor, and the recipient of its own actions. The unresolved issues from that lifetime that emerge at the life or light review set the agenda for the next incarnation.

Light, the. The light refers to the third plane of existence.

Lightbody. It is the same as the radiant body. It is the body that belongs to the third plane of conscious awareness and the visible light frequency band.

List, the. The List is the discipline taught by Ramtha where the student gets to write a list of items they desire to know and experience and then learn to focus on it in an analogical state of consciousness. The List is the map used to design, change, and reprogram the neuronet of the person. It is the tool that helps to bring meaningful and lasting changes in the person and their reality.

Make known the unknown. This phrase expresses the original divine mandate given to the Source consciousness to manifest and bring to conscious awareness all of the infinite potentials of the Void. This statement represents the basic intent that inspires the dynamic process of creation and evolution.

Mind. Mind is the product of streams of consciousness and energy acting on the brain creating thought-forms, holographic segments, or neurosynaptic patterns called memory. The streams of consciousness and energy are what keep the brain alive. They are its power source. A person's ability to think is what gives them a mind.

Mind of God. The mind of God comprises the mind and wisdom of every lifeform that ever lived on any dimension, in any time, or that ever will live on any planet, any star, or region of space.

Mirror consciousness. When Point Zero imitated the act of contemplation of the Void it created a mirror reflection of itself, a point of reference that made the exploration of the Void possible. It is called mirror consciousness or secondary consciousness. See **Self.**

Monkey-mind. Monkey-mind refers to the flickering, swinging mind of the personality.

Mother/Father Principle. It is the source of all life, the Father, the eternal Mother, the Void. In Ramtha's teachings, the Source and God the creator are not the same. God the creator is seen as Point Zero and primary consciousness but not as the Source, or the Void, itself.

Name-field. The name-field is the name of the large field where the discipline of Fieldwork^SM is practiced.

Neighborhood Walk^SM. This is the service mark of a technique created by JZ Knight for raising consciousness and energy and intentionally modifying our neuronets and set patterns of thinking no longer wanted and replacing them with new ones of our choice. This technique is exclusively taught at Ramtha's School of Enlightenment.

Neuronet. The contraction for "neural network," a network of neurons that perform a function together.

Observer. It refers to the Observer responsible for collapsing the particle/wave of quantum mechanics. It represents the great self, the Spirit, primary consciousness, the God within the human person.

Outrageous. Ramtha uses this word in a positive way to express something or someone who is extraordinary and unusual, unrestrained in action, and excessively bold or fierce.

People, places, things, times, and events. These are the main areas of human experience to which the personality is emotionally attached. These areas represent the past of the human person and constitute the content of the emotional body.

Personality, the. See **Emotional body.**

Plane of Bliss. It refers to the plane of rest where souls get to plan their next incarnations after their life reviews. It is also known as heaven and paradise where there is no suffering, no pain, no need or lack, and where every wish is immediately manifested.

Plane of demonstration. The physical plane is also called the plane of demonstration. It is the plane where the person has the opportunity to demonstrate its creative potentiality in mass and witness consciousness in material form in order to expand its emotional understanding.

Point Zero. It refers to the original point of awareness created by the Void through its act of contemplating itself. Point Zero is the original child of the Void, the birth of consciousness.

Primary consciousness. It is the Observer, the great self, the God within the human person.

Ram. Ram is a shorter version of the name Ramtha. Ramtha means the Father.

Ramaya. Ramtha refers to JZ Knight as his beloved daughter. She was Ramaya, the first one to become Ramtha's adopted child during his lifetime. Ramtha found Ramaya abandoned on the steppes of Russia. Many people gave their children to Ramtha during the march as a gesture of love and highest respect; these children were to be raised in the House of the Ram. His children grew to the great number of 133 even though he never had offspring of his own blood.

Ramtha (etymology). The name of Ramtha the Enlightened One, Lord of the Wind, means the Father. It also refers to the Ram who descended from the mountain on what is known as the terrible day of the Ram. "It is about that in all antiquity. And in ancient Egypt, there is an avenue dedicated to the Ram, the great conqueror. And they were wise enough to understand that whoever could walk down the avenue of the Ram could conquer the wind." The word Aram, the name of Noah's grandson, is formed from the Aramaic noun Araa — meaning earth, landmass — and the word Ramtha, meaning high. This Semitic name echoes Ramtha's descent from the high mountain, which began the great march.

Runner. A runner in Ramtha's lifetime was responsible for bringing specific messages or information. A master teacher has the ability to send runners to other people that manifest their words or intent in the form of an experience or an event.

Second plane. It is the plane of existence of social consciousness and the infrared frequency band. It is associated with pain and suffering. This plane is the negative polarity of the third plane of visible light frequency.

Second seal. This seal is the energy center of social consciousness and the infrared frequency band. It is associated with the experience of pain and suffering and is located in the lower abdominal area.

Secondary consciousness. When Point Zero imitated the act of contemplation of the Void it created a mirror reflection of itself, a point of reference that made the exploration of the Void possible. It is called mirror consciousness or secondary consciousness. See **Self.**

Self, the. The self is the true identity of the human person different from the personality. It is the transcendental aspect of the person. It refers to the secondary consciousness, the traveler in a journey of involution and evolution making known the unknown.

Sending-and-receiving. Sending-and-receiving is the name of the discipline taught by Ramtha in which the student learns to access information using the faculties of the midbrain to the exclusion of sensory perception. This discipline develops the student's psychic ability of telepathy and divination.

Seven seals. The seven seals are powerful energy centers that constitute seven levels of consciousness in the human body. The bands are the way in which the physical body is held together according to these seals. In every human being there is energy spiraling out of the first three seals or centers. The energy pulsating out of the first three seals manifests itself respectively as sexuality, pain, or power. When the upper seals are unlocked, a higher level of awareness is activated.

Seventh plane. The seventh plane is the plane of ultraconsciousness and the Infinite Unknown frequency band. This plane is where the journey of involution began. This plane was created by Point Zero when it imitated the act of contemplation of the Void and the mirror or secondary consciousness was created. A plane of existence or dimension of space and time exists between two points of consciousness. All the other planes were created by slowing down the time and frequency band of the seventh plane.

Seventh seal. This seal is associated with the crown of the head, the pituitary gland, and the attainment of enlightenment.

Shiva. The Lord God Shiva represents the Lord of the Blue Plane and the Blue Body®. Shiva is not used in reference to a singular deity from Hinduism. It is rather the representation of a state of consciousness that belongs to the fourth plane, the ultraviolet frequency band, and the opening of the fourth seal. Shiva is neither male nor female. It is an androgynous being, for the energy of the fourth plane has not yet been split into positive and negative polarity. This is an important distinction from the traditional Hindu representation of Shiva as a male deity who has a wife. The tiger skin at its feet, the trident staff, and the sun and the moon at the level of the head represent the mastery of this body over the first three seals of consciousness. The kundalini energy is pictured as fiery energy shooting from the base of the spine through the head. This is another distinction from some Hindu representations of Shiva with the serpent energy coming out at the level of the fifth seal or throat. Another symbolic image of Shiva is the long threads of dark hair and an abundance of pearl necklaces, which represent its richness of experience owned into wisdom. The quiver and bow and arrows are the agent by which Shiva shoots its powerful will and destroys imperfection and creates the new.

Sixth plane. The sixth plane is the realm of hyperconsciousness and the gamma ray frequency band. In this plane the awareness of being one with the whole of life is experienced.

Sixth seal. This seal is associated with the pineal gland and the gamma ray frequency band. The reticular formation that filters and veils the knowingness of the subconscious mind is opened when this seal is activated. The opening of the brain refers to the opening of this seal and the activation of its consciousness and energy.

Social consciousness. It is the consciousness of the second plane and the infrared frequency band. It is also called the image of the human personality and the mind of the first three seals. Social consciousness refers to the collective consciousness of human society. It is the collection of thoughts, assumptions, judgments, prejudices, laws, morality, values, attitudes, ideals, and emotions of the fraternity of the human race.

Soul. Ramtha refers to the soul as the Book of Life, where the whole journey of involution and evolution of the individual is recorded in the form of wisdom.

Subconscious mind. The seat of the subconscious mind is the lower cerebellum or reptilian brain. This part of the brain has its own independent connections to the frontal lobe and the whole of the body and has the power to access the mind of God, the wisdom of the ages.

Superconsciousness. This is the consciousness of the fifth plane and the x-ray frequency band.

Tahumo. Tahumo is the discipline taught by Ramtha in which the student learns the ability to master the effects of the natural environment — cold and heat — on the human body.

Tank field. It is the name of the large field with the labyrinth that is used for the discipline of The Tank®.

Tank®, The. It is the name given to the labyrinth used as part of the disciplines of Ramtha's School of Enlightenment. The students are taught to find the entry to this labyrinth blindfolded and move through it focusing on the Void without touching the walls or using the eyes or the senses. The objective of this discipline is to find, blindfolded, the center of the labyrinth or a room designated and representative of the Void.

Third plane. This is the plane of conscious awareness and the visible light frequency band. It is also known as the light plane and the mental plane. When the energy of the Blue Plane is lowered down to this frequency band, it splits into positive and negative polarity. It is at this point that the soul splits into two, giving origin to the phenomenon of soulmates.

Third seal. This seal is the energy center of conscious awareness and the visible light frequency band. It is associated with control, tyranny, victimization, and power. It is located in the region of the solar plexus.

Thought. Thought is different from consciousness. The brain processes a stream of consciousness, modifying it into segments — holographic pictures — of neurological, electrical, and chemical prints called thoughts. Thoughts are the building blocks of mind.

Torsion Process[SM]. This is the service mark of a technique created by Ramtha for raising consciousness and energy and intentionally creating a torsion field using the mind. Through this technique the student learns to build a wormhole in space/time, alter reality, and create dimensional phenomena such as invisibility, levitation, bilocation, teleportation, and others. This technique is exclusively taught at Ramtha's School of Enlightenment.

Twilight®. This term is used to describe the discipline taught by Ramtha in which the students learn to put their bodies in a catatonic state similar to deep sleep, yet retaining their conscious awareness.

Twilight® Visualization Process. It is the process used to practice the discipline of the List or other visualization formats.

Ultraconsciousness. It is the consciousness of the seventh plane and the Infinite Unknown frequency band. It is the consciousness of an ascended master.

Unknown God. The Unknown God was the single God of Ramtha's ancestors, the Lemurians. The Unknown God also represents the forgotten divinity and divine origin of the human person.

Upper four seals. The upper four seals are the fourth, fifth, sixth, and seventh seals.

Void, the. The Void is defined as one vast nothing materially, yet all things potentially. See **Mother/Father Principle.**

Yellow brain. The yellow brain is Ramtha's name for the neocortex, the house of analytical and emotional thought. The reason why it is called the yellow brain is because the neocortices were colored yellow in the original two-dimensional, caricature-style drawing Ramtha used for his teaching on the function of the brain and its processes. He explained that the different aspects of the brain in this particular drawing are exaggerated and colorfully highlighted for the sake of study and understanding. This specific drawing became the standard tool used in all the subsequent teachings on the brain.

Yeshua ben Joseph. Ramtha refers to Jesus Christ by the name Yeshua ben Joseph, following the Jewish traditions of that time.

Fig. A: The Seven Seals:
Seven Levels of Consciousness in the Human Body

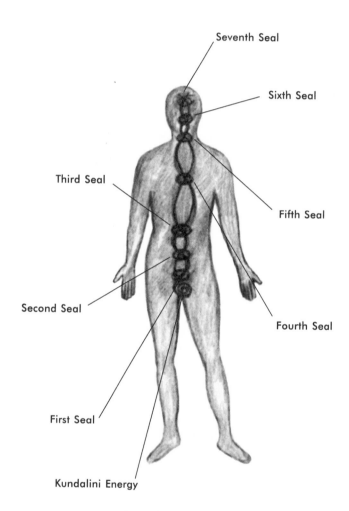

Seventh Seal

Sixth Seal

Third Seal

Fifth Seal

Second Seal

Fourth Seal

First Seal

Kundalini Energy

Fig. B: Seven Levels of Consciousness and Energy

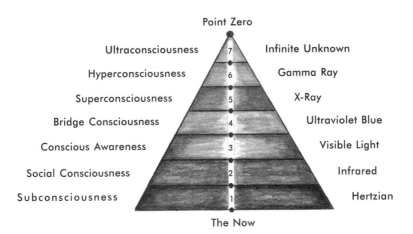

Point Zero

Ultraconsciousness	7	Infinite Unknown
Hyperconsciousness	6	Gamma Ray
Superconsciousness	5	X-Ray
Bridge Consciousness	4	Ultraviolet Blue
Conscious Awareness	3	Visible Light
Social Consciousness	2	Infrared
Subconsciousness	1	Hertzian

The Now

Copyright © 2000 JZ Knight

Fig. C: Seven Bodies Enfolded within Each Other

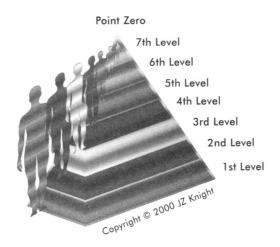

Point Zero

7th Level
6th Level
5th Level
4th Level
3rd Level
2nd Level
1st Level

Copyright © 2000 JZ Knight

FIG. D: CONSCIOUSNESS AND ENERGY IN THE LIGHT SPECTRUM

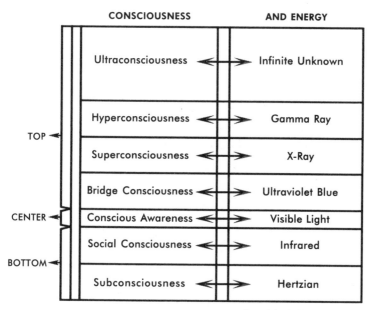

Fig. E: The Brain

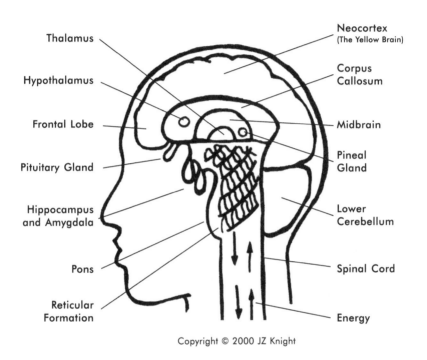

Thalamus — Neocortex (The Yellow Brain)

Hypothalamus — Corpus Callosum

Frontal Lobe — Midbrain

Pituitary Gland — Pineal Gland

Hippocampus and Amygdala — Lower Cerebellum

Pons — Spinal Cord

Reticular Formation — Energy

Copyright © 2000 JZ Knight

This is the original two-dimensional caricature-style drawing Ramtha used for his teaching on the function of the brain and its processes. He explained that the different aspects of the brain in this particular drawing are exaggerated and colorfully highlighted for the sake of study and understanding. This specific drawing became the standard tool used in all the subsequent teachings on the brain.

Fig. F: Binary Mind — Living the Image

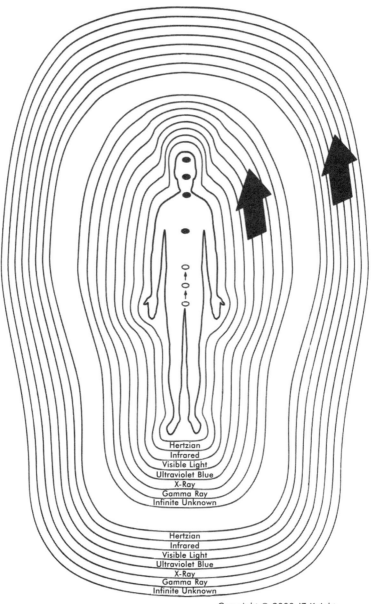

Hertzian
Infrared
Visible Light
Ultraviolet Blue
X-Ray
Gamma Ray
Infinite Unknown

Hertzian
Infrared
Visible Light
Ultraviolet Blue
X-Ray
Gamma Ray
Infinite Unknown

FIG. G: ANALOGICAL MIND — LIVING IN THE NOW

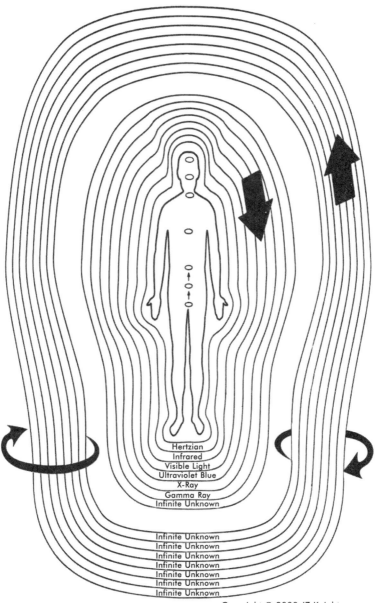

Hertzian
Infrared
Visible Light
Ultraviolet Blue
X-Ray
Gamma Ray
Infinite Unknown

Infinite Unknown
Infinite Unknown
Infinite Unknown
Infinite Unknown
Infinite Unknown
Infinite Unknown
Infinite Unknown

Fig. H: The Observer Effect and the Nerve Cell

The Observer is responsible
for collapsing the wave function of probability
into particle reality.

Particle   Energy wave   The Observer

The act of observation
makes the nerve cells fire and produces thought.

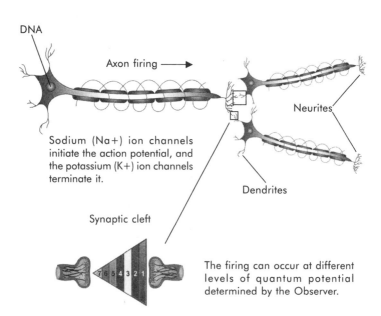

DNA

Axon firing ⟶

Neurites

Sodium (Na+) ion channels
initiate the action potential, and
the potassium (K+) ion channels
terminate it.

Dendrites

Synaptic cleft

The firing can occur at different
levels of quantum potential
determined by the Observer.

FIG. I: CELLULAR BIOLOGY AND THE THOUGHT CONNECTION

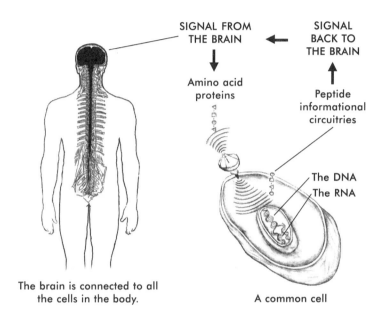

SIGNAL FROM THE BRAIN

SIGNAL BACK TO THE BRAIN

Amino acid proteins

Peptide informational circuitries

The DNA
The RNA

The brain is connected to all the cells in the body.

A common cell

Fig. J: Weblike Skeletal Structure of Mass

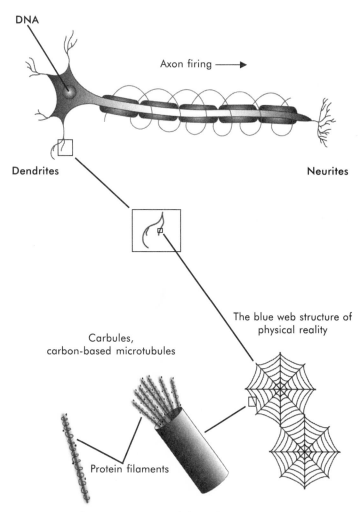

DNA

Axon firing ⟶

Dendrites

Neurites

The blue web structure of
physical reality

Carbules,
carbon-based microtubules

Protein filaments

Electrons move in and through
the protein filaments.